AF585273

Australia's Neighbours

South Korea and North Korea

DISCOVER THE COUNTRY, CULTURE AND PEOPLE

Jane Hinchey

First published 2018 by
Redback Publishing
PO Box 357 Frenchs Forest NSW 2086
Australia

www.redbackpublishing.com.au
orders@redbackpublishing.com.au

978-1-925630-29-9

Author: Jane Hinchey
Editor: Marianne Lindsell
Designer: Redback Publishing

Original illustrations © Redback Publishing 2018
Originated by Redback Publishing

Printed and bound in China by Leo Paper

Acknowledgements
Abbreviations: l—left, r—right, b—bottom, t—top, c—centre, m—middle
We would like to thank the following for permission to reproduce photographs: (Images © shutterstock) p7b Sean Pavone, p8b Jose L Vilchez, p11 BUGNUT23, p12br cjmac, p13b Son Hoang Tran, p21ml Korea.net / Korean Culture and Information Service (Photographer name) [CC BY-SA 2.0 (https://creativecommons.org/licenses/by-sa/2.0)], via Wikimedia Commons, p21mr By keizie / ⊠⊠⊠ from Seoul, Korea (DSCF3241) [CC BY 2.0 (http://creativecommons.org/licenses/by/2.0)], via Wikimedia Commons, p24 ARTRAN, p25b Panwasin seemala, p27 Loes Kieboom, p28b Chintung Lee, p29b Astrelok

Every effort has been made to contact copyright holders of any material reproduced in this book. Any omissions will be rectified in subsequent printings if notice is given to the publisher.

A catalogue record for this book is available from the National Library of Australia

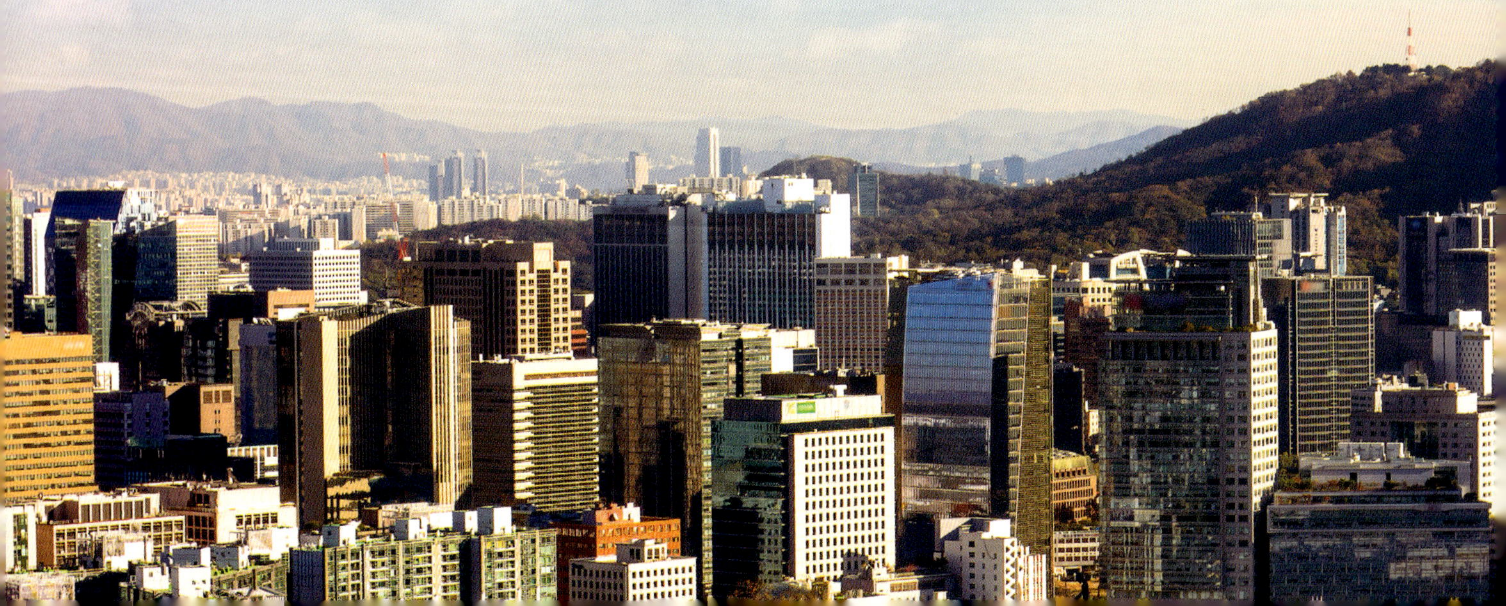

Contents

Map of South Korea	4
Snapshot	5
Meet the Neighbour: South Korea	6-7
People	8-9
Daily Life	10-13
Life in Cities	14
Life in Rural Areas	15
History	16-17
Language	18
Geography, Sustainability and Climate	19
Food and Cuisine	20-21
Religion and Beliefs	22-23
Transport	24-25
Tourism	26-27
North Korea	28-29
Flags, Symbols and Emblems	30
Find Out More	31
Glossary	32
Index	32

Map of South Korea

Snapshot

Country name: Republic of Korea (ROK), also known as South Korea
Population: 50,705,000 (2017)
Capital: Seoul
Area: 100,210 square kilometres
Official Language: Korean
Religions: Protestant, Buddhism, Catholic
Currency: South Korean Won

Fun Facts

- South Korea has the world's fastest wireless speed.
- South Koreans wear red for weddings, as a sign of good fortune.
- South Koreans say "kimchi" when taking a photo.
- South Korea is the world's largest plastic surgery market per capita.
- South Koreans are classified at birth according to blood type.

MAJOR SITES

- Seoul
- Busan
- Gyeongbokgung Palace
- Namiseom Island
- Gyeongju
- Seoraksan National Park
- The Demilitarized Zone (DMZ)

Meet the Neighbour: South Korea

South Korea is located on the southern half of the Korean Peninsula, in East Asia. North Korea lies to the north and is the only other country South Korea shares a border with. The South Korean mainland is surrounded by sea, and the coast is dotted with over 3,000 islands.

Australia and South Korea have an important partnership, which is strategically and economically aligned. South Korea's capital city, Seoul is 8,411 kilometres away from Australia's capital city, Canberra.

The first recorded contact between Australia and Korea took place when Australian missionaries arrived there in 1889. In 1904, Australian photographer George Rose spent time photographing the country and people, images that today form a valuable part of Korea's documentary history.

Over 18,000 Australian troops served under UN command during the Korean War (1950–53), and 340 died. After the war ended, the first ROK embassy was established in Australia, followed by an Australian Embassy in Seoul in 1962.

Today, the two countries have strong trade, military and diplomatic ties, and cooperate on regional security matters including the ongoing insistence that the Democratic Republic of North Korea abandon all nuclear weapons and nuclear programs. South Korea is one of Australia's largest export markets, providing ROK with essential resources and agricultural products. South Korea provides Australia with manufactured goods such as cars, telecommunications equipment and electronics.

In the 2016 census, 123,017 residents of Australia identified as having Korean ancestry. South Korea is Australia's eighth largest tourism market, and the fastest growing market, with over 280,000 South Koreans visiting Australia in 2016.

At a Glance

System of Government

South Korea is a democracy. The government has three branches: executive, legislative and judicial. A president is head of the executive branch, with a new president elected every five years. A prime minister serves under, and is chosen by, the president.

Economy

South Korea is the 11th strongest economy in the world. Family owned multinational conglomerates called chaebols, such as Samsung, Hyundai and LG Corporation dominate the country's economy.

Major Industries:

Automobiles, electronics, computers, semiconductors, televisions, shipbuilding and petrochemicals. Emerging industries include high-tech communication, internet software and services and biotechnology.

Main Agriculture:

Rice is the most important crop accounting for 90% of total grain production.

Main Exports:

Vehicles, machinery, semiconductors and ships. South Korea's main export partners are China, the United States, Hong Kong and Australia.

Main Imports:

Oil, semiconductors, natural gas and coal. South Korea's main import partners are China, Japan, the United States and Australia.

National Assembly Building

People

South Korea has a population of over 50 million people, which is the 27th largest population in the world. Most of South Korea's population is Korean. While it is seen as an ethnically homogenous country, there are also South Koreans with Chinese background. South Korea has smaller communities of other nationalities living there, including about 28,000 American troops.

Origins

Because of their geographical location, Koreans are generally considered a northeast Asian group. However, their ancestors came from the Altair Mountains, a region stretching from Siberia to the Gobi desert, and the Ural Mountains, a mountainous boundary between Europe and Asia. Tribes migrated across these areas to the Korean Peninsula.

An Aging Population

South Korea's population is aging and creating a demographic challenge. The country has a falling birth rate. In 1962 the government implemented a family planning program. More recently, statistics show that single-person households are on the rise, and people are delaying marriage. Couples are choosing to have fewer children, or even no children. Currently more than 14% of the population is aged over 65 and this will increase to 20.8% by 2026. This will place great economic strain on the healthcare system. Traditionally, each family looks after their aging relatives. However family dynamics have changed over the past few decades and aged care has become big business in South Korea.

North and South

Despite sharing the same ancient history, culture and language, North Korea and South Korea are today two separate countries. Korea was divided into two areas after the end of the Second World War. When this happened, many families lost contact with loved ones. Between 1985 and 2015, South Korea facilitated some family reunions. About 18,000 Koreans were able to meet with loved ones for a day in private and group meetings, but 66,000 other South Koreans were left on the waiting list. Many of these people were elderly and hadn't had any contact at all with their family members in North Korea. In July 2017 the new South Korean president Moon Jae-in offered to resume talks about the reunion program, but continued tension between the two countries means many elderly Koreans won't live to see their loved ones again.

Above: Prayer ribbons attached to a barbed wire fence near the border between North and South Korea

Walk in Their Shoes

How would you feel if half your family lived on one side of the country, while you lived on the other, and you were unable to ever see, call or contact them?

Daily Life

Family Life

Family is important in South Korea, however multi-generational homes are not as common as they once were. Nowadays nuclear families share small apartments, and children often live at home until they marry. While the home is still the domain of the women, this too is changing, with more and more women choosing careers over marriage and motherhood. In the past marriage, family and astrological forecasts influenced choices, but today more Koreans marry for love.

Despite the changes to the family unit, it remains the foundation of Korean society and most people continue to observe family traditions and ancestral rites. These ancestral rites are collectively known as jesa and are divided into three categories:

- Charye: held four times a year on major holidays, such as New Year
- Gije: held the night before or morning of an ancestor's death anniversary
- Sije: seasonal rights for ancestors five or more generations removed

Some other days that are important to Korean families are:

- The day a son reaches 100 days old.
- A person's sixtieth birthday.
- Mourning, both as a relative nears death, and then the responsibility of looking after ancestral graves.

Work

Work is very important to Korean people and they work hard. Many people work for large corporations, and are expected to work long hours. Data shows that in 2017, South Koreans worked the second-longest hours among member states of the Organization for Economic Cooperation and Development (OECD). While working long hours, their wages are below the average of 35 nations. South Koreans rarely take holidays, using on average only eight days of the 15 paid days they're entitled to.

Education

Education is important to South Koreans and children are expected to work hard at school. Education is universal and free through to the sixth grade. Kindergarten is optional with many families choosing to keep their children at home. From age six they begin six years of compulsory elementary education, followed by three years of middle school and three years of secondary school.

About three quarters of Korean children attend after school classes, and English classes are popular. Much of South Korea's rapid post-war growth is connected to the work ethic which starts in school. However this has resulted in enormous pressure on young people to achieve competitive results and attend top universities.

About a quarter of students choose to attend vocational schools, to study subjects such as technology, agriculture and commerce. But the majority of Korean students aim to go to university, and preparations to get into the top colleges begin as early as kindergarten.

Sport

Koreans enjoy a range of sports such as baseball, football, volleyball, table tennis, golf and archery. South Korea has some excellent ski fields and many people ski. Also popular is martial arts, especially Taekwondo. Some major sporting events have been held in South Korea, including the 1988 Summer Olympics and the Soccer World Cup in 2002, held jointly with Japan.

An Olympic Sport

Taekwondo first appeared as a demonstration sport at the 1988 Summer Olympics in Seoul, South Korea. It became a full medal sport at the 2000 Summer Olympics in Sydney.

Leisure

Young Koreans often juggle many different extracurricular activities. They learn languages, study music, play sport, watch television and play online just like young people everywhere. Western pop music is popular, but young Koreans also love their own Korean pop called K-Pop.

Music

Koreans have a strong musical history. Ancient Chinese records state that they "love to drink wine, sing and dance." Traditional Korean music has many distinct traits, from the most basic elements of the music to its tone and format. Korean folk music is complex and played by a wide range of instruments, including drums and gongs. Court music has a slow tempo.

Traditional instruments include a twelve-stringed zither called the gayageum, and a six-stringed bass zither called the geomungo.

K-Pop

South Korea's own pop music industry is booming and many children dream of K-pop stardom. It's a competitive business and stars are groomed from a young age. Children attend music, dance and singing lessons. Some children will become part of a stable of performers for major companies. These children receive gruelling training in the hope that one day they will be K-pop stars.

The Arts

South Korea's traditional arts were strongly influenced by China, however the Koreans made these arts their own.

Ceramics

Korean pottery is famous, and in the 1200s, along with tens of thousands of farmers and other artisans, some Korean master potters were kidnapped and taken to Japan in what was called the Pottery War. Celadon pottery has a blue-green tinge and was created around 1,000 years ago.

Women

Traditionally women were expected to respect and support their husbands, a submissive role that has its roots in Confucianism. The days of women being restricted by Confucian virtues are long gone. Modern Korean women are well educated, have careers and can marry for love. However there is still a strong cultural tendency to see men as the breadwinners while women are the homemakers. There is gender inequality in the workforce, politics and in daily life, but it is improving. Revisions of Korean law now provide women with equal rights to custody and property in a divorce, and more security at work. Working mothers are entitled to 90 days maternity leave, 60 of them paid. Women are also entitled to one unpaid day a month of menstruation leave.

Clothing

The hanbok is the traditional dress of South Korea. It has simple lines and bright colours. The hanbok is made up of numerous garments. Some of these are:

- Chima: a type of skirt worn with a short jacket.
- Jeogori: an upper garment for both men and women.
- Dangui: an upper garment worn by women.
- Jeonbok: a sleeveless vest worn by military personnel.
- Kkachi durumagi: a colourful overcoat worn by children.

While both men and women used to wear the hanbok, women only wear it now and usually only for special occasions.

Korean people wear western clothes now, and fashionable areas of Seoul such as Gangnam-gu and Dongdaemun-gu are filled with stores that sell both local designers and international labels.

Life in Cities

South Korea's cities, and especially the capital Seoul, are high tech, modern metropolises. Since the 1960s, the population in South Korea's cities has exploded, leading to traffic and environmental issues. Seoul has a population of just over 10 million people, making it one of the most densely populated cities in the world. It is a modern megacity, buzzing with crowds, overloaded with options for shopping and entertainment. In recent years people have flooded the capital, impacting the cost of living, especially real estate, for everyone.

Traditionally, people live in homes made of wood, but more common now are concrete houses and apartments. Modern homes are a mix of old and new, often with sparse furnishing, where families sit on heated floors, but with many western style comforts.

Cityscape of Busan

Five Largest Cities in South Korea

- Seoul
- Busan
- Incheon
- Daegu
- Daujeon

Life in Rural Areas

South Korea is a mountainous country with only 30% of its land suitable for cultivation. Rural communities struggle with aging and shrinking populations, with young people moving to cities. In 2016, only 4.9% of employed people worked in agriculture.

For those in rural communities, their way of life has not changed much for generations. Families still live in traditional style homes and own smaller farms and plots of land. Most farms produce more than one crop a year. Farmers can produce two crops of barley and rice each summer on their terraced rice fields. Other crops include soya beans, cabbage and mushrooms. As well as fruits such as apples, pears, mandarins, oranges, grapes and watermelons. Farmers who live by the sea often supplement their farming income by fishing.

Along the coast and on islands people make a living from fishing. The shallow West Sea is a fertile environment for shellfish and seaweed, while the deep seas to the east and south are better for fishing.

Homes in rural areas are larger than in cities, and usually built in the traditional style, called hanoks. These houses are positioned in relation to the land and seasons. Houses in colder regions are built to retain heat, while in warmer regions the architecture is more open-plan, in the shape of a number one.

Traditionally, Korean homes were heated with an ondol system, where heating was projected from the kitchen fire into other rooms under the floor. Today, homes are heated with modern ondol, but using gas or electricity to heat water pipes under the floor.

Traditional Korean style house

History

The ancestors of modern Koreans came from the Altair Mountains, a region stretching from Siberia to the Gobi desert, and the Ural Mountains, a mountainous boundary between Europe and Asia. Tribes migrated across these areas to the Korean Peninsula. There is archaeological evidence showing that humans lived in the region as long as 30,000 years ago.

Ancient Kingdoms

Around 2,000 years ago, three kingdoms emerged from Korea's tribal states. They were Silla, Koguryo and Pekche. The area remained this way until 668 AD when the Silla Kingdom unified Korea. The Three Kingdom Period lasted 400 years and was a time when unique cultural traditions developed. By 600 AD the Silla Kingdom had gained control of the Korean peninsula. The unified Silla period was a time of prosperity and many temples were built.

The Silla Kingdom was followed by the Koryo Kingdom, from which the name Korea comes from, in 935 and then by the Joseon Dynasty in 1392, which ruled until 1910, when Japanese colonial rule began.

Japanese Rule (1910–1945)

To Korean people, Japan's thirty-six year rule over their country was a dark time in their history. For the first ten years, Japan ruled directly through the military and any Korean dissent was crushed. By 1938, all education was in Japanese and school children were forbidden to speak Korean. Despite the heavy-handed rule, there was rapid urban growth and industrial expansion during this time. By the time the Second World War ended, and Japan surrendered, Korea was the second most industrialised nation in Asia behind Japan. This came at a high price for Koreans, who had been forced to work in Japanese factories and as soldiers during the war.

The Great Divide

Russia and the USA had agreed that Korea would be divided into two zones after the war. In August 1945 Russian troops entered the north and installed a communist government. In September, after the Japanese surrender, American troops landed in the south. Korea was then divided in two along an imaginary line, the 38th parallel. In 1948 a government was elected in the south and Korea became two countries, one communist and one democratic.

The Korean War

In 1950 North Korea invaded South Korea, and South Korea immediately asked for help from, among others, the USA and Great Britain. Sixteen countries, including Australia, came to South Korea's aid under the name of the United Nations (UN) forces. North Korea asked for help from the USSR and China.

On 27 July 1953 an armistice agreement was signed between North and South Korea. It has been in place ever since, however tensions between the two countries remain.

Two million North Koreans and 47,000 South Koreans were killed during the Korean War, along with 37,000 United Nations forces.

Australians remained in South Korea for four years after the war ended as military observers. Since then, Australia has maintained a presence discharged by the Australian Military Attaché.

Over 17,000 Australians served during the Korean War, of which 340 were killed and over 1,216 wounded. A further 29 had become prisoners of war.

Language

The Korean language is a combination of other languages such as Chinese and Japanese. Some believe its roots lie in the languages of central Asia. The modern Korean writing system, hangul, was devised in 1443 and consists of twenty-four letters.

There are officially two standard Korean dialects: the Seoul dialect in South Korea and the Phyong'yang dialect in North Korea. However there are also many regional dialects throughout both countries.

Learn the Lingo

neh: Yes
ah-nee-oh: No
jwe-song-ha-ji-mahn: Please
gahm-sah-hahm-ni-da: Thank you
chon-mahn-eh-yo: You're welcome
sil-le-hahm-ni-da: Excuse me
ahn-nyong-ha-se-yo: Good morning
ahn-nyong-hee ga-se-yo: Good-bye
ahn-nyong-ha-se-yo?: How are you?
neh jal-i-soum-ni-da: I'm fine, thank you
yong-o-rul hahl-jool asim-ni-ka?: Do you speak English?
song-ha-mi o-teo-ke dwe-si-ji-yo?: What is your name?

The Korean alphabet has 14 consonants and 10 vowels.

Geography, Sustainability and Climate

South Korea is a small country located on the Korean peninsula in East Asia. It is cut off from the mainland by North Korea. While the North Korean border is in the north, the rest of South Korea is surrounded by water: the Yellow Sea to the west, the South China Sea to the south and to the east, the East Sea (called the Sea of Japan in Japan). Unlike Japan and northern China, the Korean peninsula is geologically stable.

Only 30% of the country is farmable lowland, located mainly along the west coast. The majority of South Korea is mountainous. A granite mountain range extends down the east coast, protecting the country from typhoons and tsunami.

About 3,000 rocky islands dot the coast. The largest of these is Cheju-do, a popular holiday resort. Cheju-do is home to Korea's highest mountain, Hallasan, an extinct volcano.

Forest Rehabilitation

South Korea is one of the few countries in the world to have a successful history of forest rehabilitation. The Japanese and the Korean War devastated Korean forests, but by 2008 over 11 billion trees had been planted and now two thirds of South Korea is covered in forest. South Korea is now seen as a leader in sustainable development and sustainable forestry, and is partnering with developing countries to share its experiences of forest rehabilitation and restoration.

Climate

South Korea has a temperate climate with four distinct seasons. In winter, cold winds blow in from Mainland China and Russia. Summer can be hot and humid.

Facts and Figures

Land area: 98,480 square kilometres
Coastline: 2,413 kilometres
Highest point: Hallasan, 1,950 metres
Longest river: Nakdong, 525 kilometres

Food and Cuisine

Food is an important part of Korean culture. A traditional meal consists of rice or noodles, soup, and kimchi. Numerous side dishes will accompany a main dish. Side dishes include bean curd, meats, seaweed, seasoned vegetables and seafood. Soups contain a variety of meat and vegetables, and can range from simple broth to more complicated dishes. Koreans love bulgogi, or barbecued dishes where marinated beef is cooked over a grill.

Seasonings such as soy sauce, salt, garlic, ginger and chilli are regularly used. The presentation of food is very important. Dishes vary around the country and there are regional influences. Prior to Korea being divided into two nation states, there were eight provinces, each with its own characteristic tastes and cooking methods.

Korean cuisine has also been heavily influenced by Buddhism and family ceremonies stemming from Confucianism. The jesa ancestor rituals include food such as rice, liquor, soup, noodles, skewered meat, vegetable and fish dishes. Also on offer are dried snacks and a variety of fruit.

South Korea's National Dish

Kimchi is a spicy, pickled dish, served with most meals. It is usually made from cabbage but more than 150 kinds of kimchi are documented. The most common alternatives to cabbage are radishes, turnips and red peppers.

Traditionally women made large batches of kimchi every October, during a period called kimjang. Now, many people buy kimchi from the supermarket.

Due to the fermentation process, kimchi has many health benefits, and is now being eaten by more people for those properties in the west.

Ginseng

Ginseng is native to Korea and possibly its oldest export product. Ancient Koreans believed ginseng to be the elixir of life. Today, the government regulates the market, and Koreans drink it or take it in capsules for medicinal purposes.

On the Menu

Bipimbap:	a mixed rice bowl, with vegetables, seasoning and meat.
Bulgogi:	thinly sliced marinated beef grilled with garlic.
Japchae:	stir fried noodles with thinly shredded vegetables, sweet potato and beef.
Hoeddeok:	these sweet pancakes are a popular street food.
Soondubu jiggae:	a tofu stew with vegetables, mushrooms and sometimes beef, seafood or pork.

Korean Etiquette

If an older person hands you a drink, take it with both hands. This is a sign of respect. Also, don't start eating until the eldest male has started.

Religion and Beliefs

In ancient Korea people believed that spirits inhabited everything. All animals, plants and natural phenomena tree contain a divine spirit. There is no founder and no sacred texts for this practice, now known as animism. However some people rose to leadership roles, and they were called shamans. It was believed that the shamans could heal, dispel bad luck, and communicate with spirits. Many people still believe in animism and shamanism in Korea. While it is less popular now than Buddhism and Christianity, it is not uncommon for someone to consult a shaman if they have financial or health concerns.

In South Korea today there is complete religious freedom. Over 46% of the population have no formal religious affiliation, although they may have spiritual practices and beliefs. Christianity is the fastest growing religion in the country.

Buddhism

Arriving from China in the fourth century, Buddhism successfully merged with Korea's already developed animistic beliefs. In fact, most Buddhist temples in Korea contain a shrine dedicated to the local mountain spirit on whose land the temple sits. Buddhism was the dominant religion for centuries, until the rise of Confucianism during the Joseon Dynasty in 1392. It wasn't until after the Second World War that Buddhism once again gained acceptance. Today 23% of the population identifies as Buddhist.

Confucianism

Confucius was a philosopher from China who taught that strong family ties and respect for elders was important for society. One of his most famous sayings was, "What you do not wish for yourself, do not do to others." Followers reflect on their actions and how they affect others. The teachings of Confucius include five virtues:

- Benevolence
- Righteousness
- Propriety
- Wisdom
- Fidelity

Confucianism was introduced into Korea from China around the same time as Buddhism. In 372 AD a Confucian university was founded where Korean scholars explored the Confucian texts and from that developed Korean Confucianism.

Although very few Koreans identify as Confucian, the doctrine has influenced South Korean society profoundly.

Taoism (Daoism)

Taoism is based on the teachings of Laozi, a sixth century BC philosopher from China, and the reputed author of *Tao Te Ching*, which means 'The Way.' Although it never became one of the more popular faiths, like Confucianism it has influenced Korean society. The South Korean flag contains Taoist trigrams on it.

Christianity

Christianity first arrived in Korea in the 1500s with Confucian intellectuals, but the government banned it when new converts refused to take part in ancestral rites. By the eighteenth century Catholicism was popular with yangban families: those with knowledge of Confucian classics. But by the late 1700s Christians were being persecuted, at least 8,000 Catholics were killed and missionaries beheaded.

Despite these difficulties, Christianity took hold in Korea, thriving as a source of resistance to Japanese colonial rule. Today 29% of the population identifies as Christian. While the more conservative Protestant church has seen a decline in numbers, Catholic and Evangelical congregations are rapidly expanding.

Jeondong Catholic Church and Statue of Jesus Christ in Jeonju

Transport

South Korea has one of the most sophisticated transport systems in the world, moving people and goods all around the country. Public transport is efficient and is the preferred mode of transport for many people.

Fun Fact
South Korea is building the world's largest test site for autonomous (self-driving) cars.

Road

The country has seven highway systems. Local and state governments administer these highways, which is different to the complex expressway system, which can be privatised and are usually toll roads. South Korea is the 11th largest auto market in the world, dominated by local automobile companies like Hyundai and Kia.

South Korea has a widespread bus network, with companies that specialise in long distance routes, and regional companies that serve most towns with a local service.

Railways

The Japanese built a number of railway lines during the colonial period, but they were badly damaged during the Korean War. These were rebuilt and added to during the 1970s and 1980s and today South Korea has one of the most advanced high-speed rail systems in the world. Using this safe and convenient system, people can travel anywhere on the Korean peninsula in less than three hours.

South Korea's six largest cities also all have subway systems:

- Seoul
- Busan
- Daegu
- Gwangju
- Daejeon
- Incheon

Activity
Can you find these cities on a map?

Air

South Korea has two major airlines. Korean Air was founded by the government in 1962 but has been privately owned since 1969. Asiana Airlines launched in 1988. Both airlines serve extensive international networks. The country's main airport, Incheon International Airport, serves nearly 60 million passengers a year. There are a number of budget airlines that serve domestic and some nearby international destinations. However, with a rail system that gets travellers from one end of the country to another in less than three hours, the domestic airlines have struggled and many regional airports have closed.

Sea

South Korea is cut off from the mainland by North Korea, so it uses shipping to transport goods. It has one of the largest shipbuilding industries in the world. It also has an extensive system of ferry services operating between a number of domestic ports as well as to China and Japan.

Jeju-do Island

Tourism

Tourism is becoming a major contributor to South Korea's economy, with well over 17 million visitors in 2016. Over 45% of those visitors came from China.

Start in Seoul

South Korea's capital is a modern metropolis with an ancient heart. It contains five of the country's World Heritage sites.

- Changdeok Palace
- Hwaseong Fortress
- Jongmyo Shrine
- Namhansanseong
- the Royal Tombs of the Joseon Dynasty

Important Sites

As of 2017, there were 12 UNESCO World Heritage sites in South Korea, which make up the country's most important tourist destinations.

- 11 World Cultural Heritage Sites
- 1 World Natural Heritage Site

Can you find out what they are?

Go Island Hopping

So many islands, so little time. It's impossible to see all of South Korea's 3,000 islands, so visitors focus on a few favourites.

- Jeju-do is Korea's largest and most popular island.
- Udo Island is off Jeju Island and has black-lava cliffs.
- Jindo is connected to the mainland by a bridge, which makes it easy to get to.
- Ulleungdo has majestic scenery and traditional villages.

Visit a Folk Village

South Korean folk villages are the perfect way to learn more about the region's history and cultural traditions. There are many to choose from around the country.

Naganeupseong Folk Village

The Demilitarized Zone... A Natural Wonder

The area between South Korea and North Korea is called the Demilitarized Zone (DMZ). This strip of land is 250 kilometres long and 4 kilometres wide and is one of the most heavily militarized borders in the world, and devoid of human life. It is guarded by soldiers and surrounded by razor wire fences, land mines and artillery. No one is allowed into the DMZ. The lack of human activity in an area rich with mountains, prairies, swamps, lakes and marshes has produced the perfect conditions for wildlife to flourish. The result is one of the best-preserved environments in the world. The area stretches over a wide range of habitats, and is home to nearly 100 species of fish, approximately 45 types of amphibians and reptiles and more than 1,000 different species of insects. To date, 2,900 plant species, 70 types of mammals and 320 species of birds have been identified in the DMZ. Rare plant and fungal species flourish. Many birds stop in the DMZ as part of their annual migration. Scientists from all over the world have attended the area to study this thriving habitat and there is discussion to make the area a UNESCO biosphere reserve.

Some of the animals that call this habitat home were previously endangered. There are even stories of sightings of the endangered Siberian (Amur) tigers in the DMZ. Some other animals thriving there are:

- red-crowned cranes
- lynx
- black bears
- Amur goral
- musk deer
- Mur leopards
- spotted seals

North Korea

Snapshot

Country name:	Democratic People's Republic of Korea, also known as North Korea
Population:	50,705,000 (2017)
Capital:	Pyongyang
Area:	120,540 square kilometres
Official Language:	Korean
Currency:	North Korean Won

Flag

The flag of the Democratic People's Republic of Korea (North Korea) is red, white and blue. The wide red band stands for revolutionary spirit; the blue stands for peace, and the two white stripes represent purity. The red star in the circle represents the Korean Workers' Party, which rules the country.

National Symbol

North Korea's national symbol is the Chollima, a mythical winged horse.

Religion

North Korea is a communist state and all religion is banned.

Agriculture

The main crops grown in North Korea are rice, barley wheat, potatoes and rapeseed.

Government

North Korea has a communist government, which was ruled by Kim Il-sung for 41 years. In 1994, when he died, his son, Kim Jong-il succeeded him.

Life in North Korea

Life for the average North Korean can be difficult. Life centres on the regime, and food and basic supplies are often scarce.

Children in North Korea attend compulsory, state funded school for 10 years. The national literacy rate is 100%. Subjects such as Korean language, mathematics and literature are taught, along with more unusual subjects such as 'The childhood years of the Beloved and Respected Leader Generalissimo Kim Il-sung'. At age 10 all children join the Children's Union and read an oath of allegiance during an admission ceremony.

North Koreans become legal adults at age 17. They receive an ID and join the Kim Il-sung Socialist Youth League. North Korea has universal conscription into the military for males, and selective conscription for females. The military also provides opportunities for people to sit university entrance exams. There are more than three hundred colleges and universities in North Korea. One sixth of the population goes to university.

Great People's Study House in Pyongyang

Timeline of Key Dates in North Korea's History:

1945: Japan's colonial rule over Korea ends with its defeat in the Second World War.

1948: Korea is formally divided at the 38th parallel between the north, backed by the Soviet Union, and the south, supported by the United States.

1950-1953: The north invades the south, starting the Korean War. Approximately 2 million North Koreans died during the war.

1987-1992: North Korea develops weapons. In 1989, satellite images reveal a nuclear reprocessing plant.

1994: Founding President Kim Il-sung dies aged 82. He is succeeded by his son, Kim Jong-il.

2002: USA names North Korea as part of an 'axis of evil' in a standoff between the West and North Korea which lasts for decades.

2005: North Korea says it has nuclear weapons. It carries out its first test in October 2006.

By 2017 North Korea has tested numerous weapons and fired ballistic missiles into Japanese waters. Tensions between North Korea and the USA are at an all-time high.

Geography of North Korea

About 80% of North Korea is mountainous. The highest point, Paekdusan (2,744 metres), is an extinct volcano with a lake called Cheonji in its crater. Cheonji, which means The Lake of Heaven in English, is one of the deepest, coldest alpine lakes in the world. Legend has it that dragon-like creatures live in its waters.

North Korea's Climate: Continental, with freezing winters and humid summers.

Divided Countries Today
Officially North Korea and South Korea are still at war.

Flags, Symbols and Emblems

Flag of South Korea

The national flag of the Republic of Korea is called Taegeukgi, which means 'great extremes'. It consists of a blue and red yin-yang circle in the centre, one black trigram in each of the four corners and a white background.

The white represents peace while the yin-yang represents opposites. The trigrams are from the I Ching, an ancient Chinese divination text. On the flag they represent the four classical elements.

The flag has been used in various forms since 1883, but was officially used as the flag of South Korea on 15 October 1949.

National Emblem

The National Emblem of the Republic of Korea consists of a taegeuk surrounded by five petals. Below is the inscription, The Republic of Korea.

National Anthem

Aegukga is the national anthem of South Korea. It is also known as 'The Song of Love for the Country.'

National Animal

The national animal of South Korea is the Siberian tiger.

National Bird

The national bird of South Korea is the Korean Magpie.

Find Out More

Primary and Secondary Sources

A primary source is information created by someone who was a part of or witnessed the historical event first hand. Primary sources are very important to historians researching events and time periods. Examples of primary sources are letters, emails, filmed interviews and clips, journals and diaries, census statistics, government documents, art and maps (from the time period), the news (both print and film), photographs and maps.

A secondary source is when someone who did not actually witness the event retells the facts that someone else told them. Examples of secondary sources include news (both print and film), interviews, letters, journals and diaries, biographies, textbooks and paraphrased quotations.

Primary and Secondary Source Search

There have been a number of official reunions held between relatives living in North and South Korea. These are emotional events, usually covered by the South Korean press.

Can you find primary and secondary sources about one of these events?

Search Key Words

Seoul, Busan, South Korea, North Korea, Demilitarized Zone (DMZ), Kimchi, Samsung, Hyundai

READ BOOKS BY LINDA SUE PARK

- *When my Name was Keoko*
- *Kite Fighters*
- *SeeSaw Girl*
- *A Single Shard*

Fast Fact

Korean ceramics were so sought after that Korean master potters were kidnapped by the Japanese in the 1200s.

Glossary

BUDDHISM: a religion based on the teachings of Buddha.

COMMUNISM: an economic and social system where property and resources are collectively owned by a classless society and not by individual citizens.

CONFUCIUS: a sixth century Chinese teacher and Philosopher.

CULTURE: practices, beliefs and customs of a society or people.

DEMILITARIZED ZONE (DMZ): a strip of land running across the Korean peninsula, separating North Korea and South Korea.

ENDANGERED: when a species is at risk.

ETHNIC GROUP: people who share a common culture, language and heritage.

FOREST REHABILITATION: a coordinated effort to plant and bring back tree coverage to an area.

GINSENG: a plant with fleshy roots used for its medicinal properties.

HIGHLANDS: a mountainous or elevated region.

KIMCHI: a fermented dish that is the national dish of South Korea.

MONSOON: a season of heavy rain.

PLATEAU: large, flat area found in higher regions.

SUSTAINABILITY: to support the environment.

TEMPERATE: a mild climate.

YIN AND YANG: two opposing principles in Chinese philosophy. Yin is feminine and yang is masculine

Index

Arts, the 12
Buddhism 5, 20, 22
Christianity 22, 23
Cities 14
Climate 19, 29
Clothing 13
Confucianism 13, 20, 22, 23
Cuisine 20
Demilitarized Zone, the 5, 27, 31
Education 11
Exports 7
Flag 28, 30
Geography 19, 29
History 16, 29
Imports 7
Japanese 16, 18, 19, 23, 24, 29, 31
Korean War 6, 17, 19, 24, 29
Language 5, 18, 28
Religion 22, 28
Sport 11
Taoism 23
Tourism 26
Transport 24
Women 13